Are We Stewards of God's Creation?
Is This Our Purpose?

Many plans are in a man's mind,
but it is the LORD'S purpose for
him that will be carried out.
Proverbs 19:21

Marcella A. Spence

AuthorHouse™
1663 Liberty Drive
Bloomington, IN 47403
www.authorhouse.com
Phone: 833-262-8899

This book is printed on acid-free paper.

ISBN: 979-8-8230-3811-9 (sc)
ISBN: 979-8-8230-3813-3 (hc)
ISBN: 979-8-8230-3812-6 (e)

Library of Congress Control Number: 2024924912

Print information available on the last page.

Published by AuthorHouse 11/25/2024

authorHOUSE®

Are We Stewards Of God's Creations?
Is This Our Purpose

BY

MARCELLA A. SPENCE

Contents

PROLOGUE

THE BLESSINGS OF RIGHTEOUS LIVING

PSALMS 112

1. Praise the Lord! Hallelujah! Blessed (happy, fortunate, to be envied) is the man who fears (reveres and worships) the Lord, who delights greatly in His commandments.

2. His [spiritual] offspring shall be mighty upon earth; the generation of the upright shall be blessed.

3. Prosperity and welfare are in his house, and his righteousness endures forever.

4. Wisdom arises in the darkness for the upright, gracious, compassionate, and just who are in right standing with God.

5. It is well with the man who deals generously and lends, who conducts his affairs with justice.

6. He will not be moved forever; the uncompromisingly righteous (in right standing with God) shall be in everlasting remembrance.

7. He shall not be afraid of evil tidings; his heart is firmly fixed; trusting, leaning on and being confident in the Lord.

8. His heart is established and steady, he will not be afraid while he waits to see his desire established upon his adversaries.

9. He has given freely; he has given to the poor and needy; his righteousness (uprightness and right standing with God) endures forever; his glory shall be exalted in honor.

10. The wicked man will see it and be grieved and angered, he will grind his teeth and disappear in despair; the desire of the wicked shall perish and come to nothing.

In Matthew 5:48 Jesus commands us: You, therefore, MUST be perfect, growing into complete maturity of godliness in mind and character, having reached the proper extreme of virtue and integrity, as your heavenly Father is perfect. We hear many preachers say that we are not perfect. It is not that we are not perfect, it is that we are striving to be perfect. Jesus was perfect and we are made perfect to Jehovah Father through Jesus. Jesus overcame the world and conquered it for you. John 16:3

EXERCISE: Do you imitate the qualities of the righteous? Write a list of 10 things/ways that you believe in which you are righteous. Then, make a list of 20 things or times in which you are in conformity as to the profile of the righteous. What are some examples you remember from the Bible?

Notes:

_____

_____

_____

_____

_____

JESUS THE STEWARD

The stewardship of Jesus is exemplified through His life, teachings, and ultimate sacrifice, revealing principles of responsibility, service, and care for God's creation and people. Here are some key aspects of Jesus' stewardship.

1. SERVANT LEADERSHIP

Jesus modeled servant leadership, showing that true greatness is found in serving others, not in being served. He washed His disciples' feet to demonstrate humility and care (John 13:3-17), saying, "For even the Son of Man did not come to be served, but to serve, and to give his life as a ransom for many" (Mark 10:45).

2. FAITHFULNESS TO GOD'S MISSION

Jesus was entrusted with the mission of salvation, which He faithfully completed through obedience to the Father. This is reflected in His prayer: "I have brought you glory on earth by finishing the work you gave me to do" (John 17:4). His parable of the talents (Matthew 25:14-30) emphasizes being faithful stew-ards of what God has entrusted to us.

3. STEWARDSHIP OF CREATION

In Matthew 6:26-30, Jesus acknowledges the beauty and provision in creation, teaching us trust in God's care. This reminds us of our responsibility as stewards of the earth. Genesis 1:26-30

4. GENEROSITY AND COMPASSION

Jesus showed generosity and compassion of caring for the poor, feeding the hungry, and healing the sick. He multiplied loaves and fish to feed thousands (Matthew 14:13-21), showing not only His power but also His heart for concern in sharing resources.

5. ULTIMATE SACRIFICE FOR HUMANITY

The greatest act of stewardship is Jesus' sacrifice on the cross for the redemption of humanity. He gave His life freely, stewarding the gift of grace, so that others may have eternal life (John 3:16). His stewardship wasn't just about material or earthly matters but was also spiritual and eternal.

6. JESUS' TEACHING ON ACCOUNTABILITY

In the parable of the unfaithful steward (Luke 16:1-13), Jesus teaches that we are accountable for how we manage what God has given us. This includes material wealth and opportunities to serve God and others.

Through these acts and teachings, Jesus demonstrates the principles of stewardship—faithfulness, service, generosity, care for creation, and accountability—all rooted in love and obedience to God.

STEWARD OF THE GOSPEL

When you decided to accept Jesus as Lord of your life did you know that you are now a steward of the Gospel? So now that you know this, are you a true steward of the Gospel?

Stewardship is the position of a steward. A steward is a person in charge of a large estate or an administrator of finances or property according to the Webster's New World Dictionary and Thesaurus. Another name for steward is trustee. So, what makes a good steward? I chose these two examples in the bible as references: Eliezer, Abraham's servant, and the centurion's servant.

In Genesis 24 we meet Eliezer of Damascus who was the eldest servant of Abraham. He ruled over all that Abraham had. As you know, Abraham was extremely wealthy, so Eliezer had a great responsibility. Verse 2 states that Eliezer was dependable and trustworthy. Abraham didn't have to look over Eliezer's shoulder to see if he was doing right. Then verse 12 states that Eliezer was a praying man. This example tells us that Eliezer prayed constantly, that he remained in the graces of not only his master but in the graces of God. Further down you will see an example of the previous sentence. Verse 27, Eliezer gave God thanks and praises always and at any time. This is something we are constantly told to do. Verse 33, Eliezer put his master's business first. Before he ate the food that Laban placed before him, he told Laban of the business of his master Abraham. Verse 35, He never spoke of any concerns of himself, only of his master Abraham's business. If you go back even in prayer and praises, it was about Abraham. Most important, Eliezer worshiped God and gave God the glory. All that Eliezer did are the characteristics of a model servant of God.

The Characteristics of a Model Servant of God

#1. Dependable and trustworthy.
#2. A praying person.
#3. Gives Jehovah thanks and praises
always and anytime.
#4. Puts Kingdom business first.
#5. Never speaks of self but of God.
#6. Worships God and gives God the glory.

Now where do you think Eliezer learned how to do this? He had a great example to follow. John 15:20 states that a servant is not greater than his Master. A servant does what he is told to do. We are a Christian steward, commissioned to do our Master, Jesus' bidding. If the leader keeps Jehovah's Word and obeyed the Jesus' teaching, the disciple must also keep and obey The Word and Jesus' teachings.

When Moses was called to serve in the assignment given to him by God, God instructed him to go to the elders of Israel with the message He gave him. The Bible gives precise descriptions for those who are in church leadership positions and how they are expected to function and live. The faithful stewards' first responsibility is to Jehovah alone. In Acts, when the Apostles were arrested and put on trial for preaching about Jesus and were told by the council to stop preaching about Jesus they responded as such; Then Peter and the other apostles replied, we ought to obey God rather than men. (Acts 5:26-29) Regardless of title and position doing things Jehovah's way should be first.

Another person is the centurion's bondservant in Luke 7. He was honored and highly valued by his master, the centurion, a high-ranking officer of the Roman Legion. This centurion who had many demands which he had to adhere to and who spent much of his time away from home needed someone who fit the characteristics of a model servant of God. He may not have looked at it in that way but that is what he needed. His servant obviously fit the requirements, for when the servant became gravely ill, he commanded the Jewish elders to go to Jesus so that Jesus may heal his servant. Just from the centurion's actions, we see that he did not want to lose this good servant. He also knew that Jesus was able to heal him.

COMPARISON OF ELDER
& STEWARD/TRUSTEE

<u>**ELDER**</u>
Chosen to serve in a spiritual capacity.
(In the Bible was of a Jewish Sect)
Has spiritual gift(s):
Teaching, Counsel, Exhort, etc.
Was to be respected by all
(1 Timothy 4:6-5:3)
First Responsibility is to God

<u>**STEWARD/TRUSTEE**</u>
Chosen to serve by
minister/body of the Church.
(Serving in matters of
financing/administration etc.)
Known as bondservants in the Bible.
-- has the ability to manage large households
Responsibility to his master.
A good steward was held in honor
and highly valued. Luke 7:2
First responsibility is to God.

A FAITHFUL STEWARD

What are the criteria of a faithful steward? Stewardship in the biblical sense is the responsibility to manage, protect, and use wisely what belongs to God. This responsibility carries a spiritual obligation: to manage these affairs as God would, recognizing that we are ultimately caretakers, not owners. It reflects the belief that everything we have—our time, resources, gifts, talents, and even the people or property entrusted to us—ultimately belongs to God. This means using the resources in a way that honors and benefits the true owner, ensuring the well-being and needs of those for whom we are responsible. As stewards, we are called to care for these blessings faithfully, keeping in mind that our role is one of **service**, not ownership. For those who have been placed in charge of our spiritual well-being, to teach and provide wisdom and knowledge, remember to be true to the Word of Jehovah. Do not let your traditions, culture, emotions or ego overtake your first responsibility that is to God.

And the Lord said, "Who then is that faithful steward, the wise man whom his master will set over those in his household service to supply them their portion of rest at the appointed time?" Luke 12:42

The Bible outlines several qualities and criteria that characterize a **FAITHFUL STEWARD**, especially for those in leadership positions. The key qualities are:

Trustworthiness and Integrity ~ It is required of stewards that they be found trustworthy. (1 Corinthians 4:2) A faithful steward is reliable, honest, and upholds the truth. Integrity means doing what is right, even when no one else is watching, and being faithful to one's responsibilities.

Humility and Accountability ~ Obey your leaders and submit to them, for they are keeping watch over your souls, as those who will have to give an account. (Hebrews 13:17) Biblical stewardship involves being humble, recognizing that we are caretakers of what is not our own. We are accountable to God and should make decisions with reverence and humility, understanding that we will give an account for how we managed His resources.

Wisdom and Diligence ~ Who then is the faithful and wise servant, whom his master has set over his household? (Matthew 24:45) Stewardship requires careful planning, insight, and diligent work. A faithful steward uses resources effectively and avoids waste, maximizing the potential of what has been entrusted.

Generosity and Selflessness ~ As each has received a gift, use it to serve one another, as good stewards of God's varied grace. (1 Peter 4:10) Faithful stewards use their gifts to benefit others, freely giving of their time, talents, and resources to serve those around them. This reflects God's generosity and love.

Respect for the Owner's Wishes ~ A steward remembers that their role is not about personal gain or preferences but about respecting the owner's inten-tions and desires for the property or people under their care.

As each of you has received a gift (a special spiritual talent, a gracious divine endowment), employ it for one another as befits good trustees of God's many-sided grace; faithful stewards of the extremely diverse powers and gifts granted to Christians by unmerited favor. Whoever speaks, let him do it as one who utters oracles of God; whoever renders service, let him do it as with the strength which God furnishes abundantly, so that in all things Jehovah may be glorified through Jesus Christ the Messiah. To Him be the glory and dominion forever and ever, through endless age. Amen. (So be it). 1 Peter 4:10-11

Scripture references: Qualified elders should be as follows: These elders should be men who are of unquestionable integrity, are irreproachable, the husband of <u>one</u> wife, whose children are well trained and are believers, not open to the accusation of being loose in morals, conduct or unruly, disorderly. For the minister, as Jehovah's steward, must be blameless, not self-willed, arrogant, presumptuous; he must not be quick tempered or given to drink, quarrelsome; he must not be confiscating, greedy for financial gain; But he must be hospitable (loving and a friend to believers, strangers and foreigners); he must be a lover of good, (of people and things) sober-minded, upright, fair minded, a devout man, religiously correct, temperate, keeping himself in order. He must hold fast to the sure, trustworthy Word of God as he was taught it, so that he may be able both to give inspiring instructions and encouragement in sound doctrine and to refute, convict those who contradict, oppose it showing the wayward their error. Titus 1:6-9

So then, let us apostles be looked upon as ministering servants of Christ and stewards (trustees) of the mysteries (the secret purposes) of God. 1 Cor. 4:1 But refuse, avoid irreverent legends (profane and impure and godless fictions, mere grandmothers' tales) and silly myths, express your disapproval of them. Train yourself toward godliness (piety), keeping yourself spiritually fit. For physical training is of some value (useful for a little), **but godliness, spiritual training is useful and of value in everything, in every way, for it holds promise for the present life and for the life which is to come.** This saying is reliable, worthy of complete acceptance by everybody. With a view of this, we toil and strive, because we have fixed our hope on the living God, who is the Savior of all men, especially of those who believe (trust in, rely on, and obey Him). Continue to command these things and to teach them. Let no one despise, think less of you because of your youth, but be an example for the believers in speech, in conduct, in love, in faith, and in purity. Till I come, devote yourself to public and private reading, to exhortation and to teaching, revealing partially doctrine. Do not neglect the gift which is in you, that special inward quality which was directly imparted to you by the Holy Spirit by prophetic utterance when the elders laid their hands upon you at your ordination. Practice, cultivate, meditate upon these duties; throw yourself wholly into them as your ministry, so that your progress may be evident to everyone. Look well to yourself [to your <u>personality</u>] and to your teaching; persevere in these things [hold to them], for by so doing you will save both yourself and those who hear you. Do not sharply censure, rebuke an older man, but earnestly ask, plead with him as you would with a father. Treat younger men like brothers; Treat older women like mothers and younger women like sisters, <u>in all purity.</u> Always treat with great consideration, give aid to those who are truly widowed. 1 Timothy 4:7-5:3

In modern terms, stewardship is often called Guardianship, Power of Attorney, Trusteeship, or similar roles, where someone is given legal responsibility over another's property, finances, or welfare.

In context, biblical stewardship is a call to reflect God's values in every decision, with respect, care, and love for His creation, managing all we have with a servant's heart. This involves aligning actions with God's purpose.

<u>If you lay all these instructions before the brethren, you will be a worthy steward and a good minister of Jesus Christ, ever nourishing your own self on the truths of the faith and of the good Christ-like instruction which you have closely followed. 1 Timothy 4:6</u>

EARTHLY STEWARDSHIP

After God created the heavens, the living earth, the creatures, and man, He gave to mankind command as the steward over it all. This command continues to be handed down to all generations of mankind. Even though we are born in sin we are blessed from birth and given creation authority to be fruitful, to multiply and fill the earth. Putting also under our authority, the care and rule of all the animals of the air and every living thing that moves on the earth. We need to be more diligent in caring for the earth. Genesis 1.

Do you realize that since the days of the building of the Tower of Babel mankind has not been in complete harmony with one another? So, what is true harmony? Before I answer that question, reflect on all that has transpired throughout the ages. Even today there are constant conflicts. Conflicts designed to keep our minds busy and occupied from focusing on Jehovah Father and Jesus. However, today are exactly the times when you need to focus on Them. To name a few; wars, diseases, viruses, discrimination, prejudices, identity crises etc. There so many more but realize and focus on the ones that are subtle. The ones that Satan deceives us into believing are important. The newest ones are the lies about gender identification and disconnection of our spirit from God (non-binary). So, back to harmony. Grace and spiritual peace be yours from God our Father and the Lord Jesus Christ. May blessing be to the God who has blessed us in Christ in the heavenly realm. In His Love God chose us, picked us out Himself as His own (Gen. 1:27-created) in Christ (Gen. 2:7-formed) that we should be holy and blameless in His sight before Him in Love. (John 3:16) For God planned in love for us (Romans 5:8) to be revealed as His own children through Jesus Christ (Rom. 8:15-17) according to the purpose of His will (Rom. 8:28-30) to the praise and care of His Grace which God so freely bestowed on us in Jesus. (Ephesians 2:8) In Jesus we have redemption through His blood, forgiveness of our shortcoming and trespasses in harmony and unity with the riches and the generosity of His Grace. (Ephesians 2:8) Which He marked upon us in every kind of wisdom and understanding, making known to us the secret of His will.

HARMONY IN JESUS

And it is this: In harmony and unity with good pleasure which He had previously settled and set forth in Jesus. In Jesus we also were made God's heirs, and we gained possession of an inheritance; for we have been predestined in harmony and unity with His goal, who works out everything in harmony and balance with the guidance and plan of His own will. So that we who first put our confidence in Jesus have been destined and appointed to live for the praise of His glory! In Jesus you also have heard the word of Truth, the Gospel of your salvation, believed in, obeyed to, relied on Him, were stamped with the seal of the Holy Spirit. The Spirit is the down payment of our heirship, in hope of its full redemption, our taking complete possession of it---to the praise of His Glory. And so that you can know and understand what is the immeasurable, unlimited, exceeding greatness of God's power in us, for us who believe, as shown in the working of His mighty strength. For it is by free grace that you are saved through your faith. And this salvation is not of yourselves, it is the gift of God. Not because of the fulfillment of the Law's demands, lest any man should boast. It is not the result of what anyone can possibly do, so no one can pride himself in it or glory in himself. (Ephesians 1:2-9, 11-14, 19; 2:8-9)

PARENTAL STEWARDSHIP

Parental stewardship involves the responsibility of parents to care for, nurture, guide, and spiritually lead their children. Christian parents are entrusted with the task of raising their children in alignment with God's will, ensuring their physical, emotional, and spiritual well-being.

1. TEACHING & INSTRUCTING IN GOD'S WAY

Christian parents are called to instruct their children in the ways of the Lord, guiding them with biblical principles so that they can grow in faith and wisdom. Proverbs 22:6 says, "Train up a child in the way he should go, and when he is old, he will not depart from it." This highlights the long-term impact of spiritual and moral instruction. Also, in Deuteronomy 6:6-7, parents are commanded to diligently teach God's commandments to their children: "These commandments that I give you today are to be on your hearts. Impress them on your children. Talk about them when you sit at home and when you walk along the road, when you lie down and when you get up." This teaches the importance of integrating faith into everyday life.

2. PROVIDING DISCIPLINE WITH LOVE

Discipline is an essential part of parental responsibility. Guiding children to make wise decisions and understand the consequences of their actions. Proverbs 13:24 states, "Whoever spares the rod spoils their children, but the one who loves their children is careful to discipline them." This shows that <u>loving discipline</u> is necessary to help children grow into responsible and moral adults. Likewise, Ephesians 6:4 gives further instruction, saying, "Fathers, do not provoke your children to anger, but bring them up in the discipline and instruction of the Lord." Parents are to discipline with love, not harshness, so as not to lead their children to frustration or resentment.

3. PROVIDING FOR PHYSICAL & EMOTIONAL NEEDS

Stewardship also includes ensuring children's physical well-being by providing for their needs, such as food, shelter, education, and safety. 1 Timothy 5:8 teaches, "Anyone who does not provide for their relatives, and especially for their own household, has denied the faith and is worse than an unbeliever." Parents are entrusted with the duty of provision and care for their family. Today, this extends beyond just material provision. Emphasizing the importance of emotional support, security, and fostering a loving environment where children feel valued and supported.

4. MODELING GODLY CHARACTER & INTEGRITY

Children learn by observing their parents, making it essential for parents to model godly character, integrity, and kindness in their daily lives. Titus 2:7 encourages believers to "set an example by doing what is good. In your teaching show integrity, seriousness, and soundness of speech." This applies to parents who are to reflect Christ's character in their own actions. Parents today are also encouraged to live out values like honesty, compassion, hard work, and humility, creating a household culture that reinforces these qualities in their children.

5. PRAYING FOR & WITH THEIR CHILDREN

Prayer is a powerful tool in parental stewardship. In James 5:16, the Bible speaks of the power of prayer: "The prayer of a righteous person is powerful and effective." Parents should not only pray for their children's protection and guidance but also teach their children how to pray, fostering a relationship between the child and God.

6. NURTURING INDIVIDUALITY & GIFTS

Children are unique, and parental stewardship includes helping them discover and develop their God-given gifts. Proverbs 22:6 can also be understood as encouraging parents to "train up a child according to their way," meaning parents should nurture their children's unique abilities and callings. This means, recognizing the individuality of each child, supporting their interests, and providing them with opportunities to grow their talents, while ensuring those gifts are used to honor God.

7. PREPARING CHILDREN FOR INDEPENDENCE

Parents are also tasked with equipping their children to become independent, capable, and contributing members of society. Jesus alludes to this principle in Luke 16:10 when He says, "Whoever can be trusted with very little can also be trusted with much." This principle can also apply to parental stewardship in teaching children responsibility and accountability.

PARENTAL STEWARDSHIP IN CONTEXT

Parental stewardship is about more than just providing basic needs; it's about shaping character, fostering faith, promoting healthy relationships, and preparing children to fulfill their purpose in life. This includes navigating the complexities of modern-day life—social media, technology, and the ever-evolving societal norms—while maintaining the core biblical principles of love, discipline, instruction, and faith.

Parents, you are ultimately accountable to God for how you raise your children. You are called to guide them with wisdom, grounded in Scripture, while showing grace and unconditional love, just as God shows His children.

ELIEZER OF DAMASCUS

THE CHARACTERISTICS OF
A FAITHFUL STEWARD

GENESIS 24

Eliezer of Damascus was the eldest servant of Abraham who ruled over all that Abraham possessed.

Characteristic #1

Eliezer was dependable and trustworthy.

Verse 2: And Abraham said to the eldest servant of his house [Eliezer of Damascus], who ruled over all that he had, I beg of you, put your hand under my thigh; …

Characteristic #2

Eliezer was a praying man.

Verse 12: And he said, O Lord, God of my master Abraham, I pray You, cause me to meet with good success today, and show kindness to my master Abraham.

Characteristic #3

Eliezer gave God thanks and praises always and anytime.

Verse 26-27: The man bowed down his head and worshipped the Lord And said, Blessed be the Lord, the God of my master Abraham, who has not left my master bereft (*unhappy in love*), destitute (*lacking*) of His loving-kindness and steadfastness. As for me, going on the way of obedience and faith the Lord led me to the house of my master's kinsmen.

Characteristic #4

Eliezer puts kingdom business first.

Verse 33: A meal was set before him, but he said, I will not eat until I have told of my errand. And Laban said, Speak on.

Characteristic #5

Eliezer never spoke of himself but of his master Abraham.

Verse 34-35: And he said, I am Abraham's servant. And the Lord has blessed my master mightily, and he has become great; and He has given him flocks, herds, silver, gold, menservants, maidservants, camels and asses.

Characteristic #6

Eliezer worshipped God and gave God glory.

Verse 48: And I bowed down my head and worshipped the Lord and blessed the Lord, the God of my master Abraham, who had led me in the right way to take my master's brother's daughter to his son.

WHO IS THE LORD OF YOUR LIFE?

So, you ask the question, how can I be a good steward? Finally, to excel at stewardship in Christianity, you must decide who is the Lord of your life. Who is it that you are following? Have you fully submitted your life to Jesus Christ and committed to His model? Is Jesus your source?

ISAIAH calls us to regard **Jesus,** the Lord of Hosts as holy. Honor His holy name by regarding Him as your only hope of safety, let Him be your fear and let Him be your dread so you don't offend Him by your fearing man and distrusting Him. When you do this, He will be your sanctuary---a sacred and indestructible refuge as promised in Matthew 16:18. To those who reject Jesus, He will become a stumbling and a rock of offense.

Isaiah also warned that when people turn away from trusting in Jehovah and seek guidance from mediums and wizards, they are straying from God. He directs them to the teaching and testimony of God's Word, reminding us, if someone's teachings do not align with the Word, it's because they lack spiritual maturity.

Despite their waywardness, the people do not return to the One who smote them, nor do they seek or inquire of Him as their essential need. For this, God's anger remains, and His hand is still stretched out in judgement. When Jesus completes His work if chastisement and purification on Mount Zion and Jerusalem, He will punish the arrogant and prideful, making a full end of their deeds. What will you do on that day? Isaiah 8:13-14, 16,19; 9:12b-13, 19- 20; 10:12

Jesus Christ should be the **Lord** of your life. He has prepared for you a counselor, a comforter and a guide. You must acknowledge His **Lordship**. How do you do this? By confessing:

> **"I AM A BORN-AGAIN CHILD OF GOD.**
> **THE HOLY SPIRIT DWELLS WITHIN ME**
> **I DO NOT WALK ACCORDING**
> **TO THE FLESH BUT BY THE HOLY SPIRIT."**

JEHOVAH the FATHER is a SPIRIT (A Spiritual Being) and those who worship Him must worship in Spirit and in Truth. John 4:24

MY CONFESSION OF:
MY LIFE IN THE SPIRIT

ROMANS 8:1-17, 26-39
(Read Daily)

I am of Jesus Christ. I am freed from the law of sin and death. I do not live or move in the ways of the flesh but in the manner of living of the Holy Spirit. I am controlled by the guiding rule of the Holy Spirit and my mind is set and seek those things of the Holy Spirit.

My mind, it is life and soul peace both now and forever. I am living the life of the Holy Spirit of Jehovah who dwells within me, who directs and controls me and restores to life my mortal body through His Spirit.

My natural body is dead by reason of sin and guilt and my spirit is alive because of the righteousness that He credits to me. **I am a child of God** because I am led by His Spirit. God's Spirit is not a spirit of slavery to put me in fear, but I have received the Spirit of adoption. God's Spirit testifies with my own spirit assuring me that I am a child of God, heir of God and fellow heir with Jesus, sharing in His inheritance and His sufferings if I am to share His Glory.

The Holy Spirit comes to my aid and bears me up in my weaknesses. I do not know what prayer to offer or how to offer it worthily as I ought, but the Holy Spirit Himself goes to meet my supplication and plead on my behalf with unspeakable yearns and groaning too deep for utterance. God searches my heart and knows what is in the mind of the Holy Spirit, what His intent is, because the Spirit intercedes and pleads before God in my behalf according to and in harmony with God's will.

I am assured and know that God being a partner in my labor that all things are working together and is fitting into a plan for my good because I love God and am called according to His design and purpose. Jehovah foreknew me and is aware and loves me. He has destined me from the beginning to be molded into the image of His Son Jesus. Since He foreknew me, He also called me and justified me, putting me into right standing with Him. I am also glorified.

For if God is for me who can be against me? Who can be my foe if God is on my side? He who did not withhold or spare His own Son but gave Him up for me and with Him (Jesus) freely and graciously give me all other things. Who can bring any charge against God's elect when it is God who justifies? Who will come forward and accuse and impeach me whom God has chosen? Not God, for He has acquitted me. Who will condemn me? Not Jesus, the Messiah, who died and was raised from the dead who is now at the right hand of God pleading on my behalf.

No one or anything will be able to separate me from the love of God. For God's sake I am put to the manner of living of all human nature all day long. I am looked at, considered as defenseless for the manner of living of all human nature. Yet amid all these things I am more than a conqueror and gain a surpassing victory through God who loves me.

For I know that neither death nor life, nor angels nor principalities, nor things impending and threatening nor things to come, nor powers, nor heights, nor depth nor anything else in all creation will be able to separate me from the love of God which is in Christ Jesus my Lord. Amen (so be it).

REFLECTION TIME!

PLEASE TAKE TIME TO REFLECT ON YOUR LIFE. ASK YOURSELF & GOD: AM I A FAITHFUL SERVANT OF GOD? WHAT ARE THE CHANGES FOR ME TO MAKE?

NOTES: WRITE THEM DOWN. CHECK YOUR NOTES DAILY TO SEE WHAT YOU CAN DO EACH DAY. PRACTICE MAKES PERFECT. DEVELOP NEW GODLY HABITS AND BE CONSISTENT!

The next two pages have templates to help you started on reflecting your daily thoughts and actions. Let this help to guide you with steps in self-love so that you can love others. Begin each week by filling out (make copies as needed) each form and at the end of the week check back to see what you have accomplished.

Ways I Can
LOVE MYSELF
C H E C K L I S T

○

○

○

○

○

○

○

WORKOUT/EXERCISE/DIET

○ CARDIO   ○ WEIGHT   ○ YOGA

○ STRETCH   ○ REST DAY   ○ OTHER

THINGS THAT MADE ME HAPPY TODAY

HOURS OF SLEEP   (Hours)

1 2 3 4 5 6 7 8

WATER BALANCE   (Glass)

1 2 3 4 5 6 7 8

MOOD

ANGRY   TIRED   SAD   GREAT   FUN

Weekly Reflections

Focus

Goals

Highlights

Improvement

Personal Growth

Things I am Grateful

Important Notes

ABOUT THE AUTHOR

When I first began writing this book, I considered the title Stewardship at Work. However, that didn't quite capture the heart of what I felt led to share. As I always do, I turned to God for guidance. In response, God directed me to reflect deeply on my journey, the places I've been, and the people I've encountered from all walks of life. I paid close attention to their stories—their struggles, beliefs, and ways of living—whether they were homeless, working, or business owners.

A pivotal experience in my understanding of stewardship came when I was entrusted with caring for my mother and father during the last months of their lives. As a mother myself, I became like a mother to my own parents, caring for them with the same devotion I give my children. Later, I found myself caring for my brother, whom I hadn't seen in 40 years, after he was severely injured. Although we didn't have much time together before he passed, this experience taught me a great deal about family, forgiveness, and faith.

In the years since, I've had the joy of becoming a grandmother and the opportunity to live and travel to various places. I have witnessed firsthand how, despite differences in background and culture, people are remarkably alike in facing life's challenges. What ultimately shapes us is how we respond to these challenges based on our beliefs.

Through all these experiences, I've come to understand that our ultimate purpose is to fulfill God's will and the unique calling He has set before us. This book is a reflection of that journey, a testimony of how God's purpose becomes clearer when we view our lives through the lens of stewardship.

Are We Stewards of God's Creations?
Is This Our Purpose?

There are so many circumstances and people that you encounter during your lifetime on this planet, and we are often times oblivious to them. The joys, the sorrows and chaos we remember them but for a moment. The problem is that we want to see the answer to our prayers. We shouldn't wait for something to happen to pray or participate but make it a daily habit to pray for those around us and around the world. Some of us get involved either with hands-on or by giving or praying. Faith is a fundamental truth in Christianity. We must obey, completely trust Jehovah Father, believe in and rely on Jesus with your prayers and obey the Holy Spirit's guidance. They always know best the where, when, and how to apply your prayers. Being a faithful steward is one of the processes of your purpose. I hope that this book will help you to be a faithful steward. Marcella A. Spence